Flights of Faith a

A poetry collection by Brenda E. Lynch

PreeTa Press

Brenda E. Lynch – an introduction.

I first met Brenda in 2004, in a professional capacity. I worked for the ambulance service then, and I used to take her for day care at Fairfield Hospital in Bury.

Brenda has suffered from bouts of severe depression throughout most of her adult life. Despite her health problems, she has always been a keen artist and has had a strong interest in classical music, which we often discussed on our hospital trips. She later showed me some of her paintings, which I admired very much.

Brenda was born in Enfield, Middlesex in 1931, and left school aged 14. One of her earliest jobs was working in the BBC gramophone library, where she came into contact with Sir Adrian Boult. She later worked in hospitals – she recalls that one day she was in the appointments department at Great Ormond Street Children's Hospital when she noticed Prince Charles, who had come to have his tonsils out! Brenda later trained for a nursing career but her health issues had a detrimental impact on her working life.

Brenda and her husband Frank, who was originally from Liverpool, first met at a discussion group in London about Catholic education. They married on June 1st 1967, and celebrated their fiftieth wedding anniversary in 2017.

Shortly after they married, Frank changed career from engineering to teaching and they moved north to Radcliffe. Frank was a keen amateur actor, having appeared in more than 30 plays in the North West area. He also appeared on television - once on

Fifteen To One, and twice on Mastermind. Frank was always supportive of Brenda's artistic activities.

It was only recently I discovered Brenda had a talent for poetry. Brenda had heard that I wrote, and one day I was passed a piece she had half-written, asking if I could finish it. I was able to do so and performed the resulting piece in public on her behalf, to a good reception. I was later intrigued to receive a small exercise book, full of hand-written poems, which Brenda asked me to look at. This was joined later by a second exercise book - so many poems that I enlisted the help of my dear friend and colleague Eve Nortley. Eve and I were so impressed by the rich imagery and powerful emotion of Brenda's words that we quickly decided that more people really should see her work.

Sadly, Frank passed away on 7th October 2017, before this book was ready. However he did see an early draft and we have incorporated his suggestions in this, the final version.

The result is this volume of poetry, "Flights of Faith And Feeling", which we are honoured to have helped publish. Brenda's Christian faith is evident in much of her writing; but there are also powerful themes of loss, love, and the beauty of the natural world. We feel sure that, whatever your beliefs, you will be moved and uplifted by the words of this hitherto undiscovered writer.
Chris Bainbridge, Bury, March 2018.

Published in 2018 by
Preeta Press, Bolton, Greater Manchester
preetapress.com

Front, Back cover and inner photographs by Chris Bainbridge
ISBN: 9781999848965

Printed by Printdomain Ltd,

Acknowledgements

Special thanks to Chris Bainbridge and Eve Nortley for collating this book.
Photographs and Cover designs by Chris Bainbridge.

Original picture by Brenda E. Lynch

Contents

A House Divided

In just one eye blink of time
You came
Where from? And died.
Where now do you hide?
Oh Christ – re-crucified.
Until you are Lord of me,
I will never be free.
We pretend that you never came,
That this lovely world and all its powers
Are ours.
But will it ever be so?
Do not sleep now, weep now!
And be reconciled.
We who are called out of time
In love's own name
See the havoc that our greed has made.
Clinging to mere printed words
Turns hands into claws,
Plough shares into swords
Brother against brother
Even this love prophesized
That our fiercest enemy would be in our own house,
So the mighty God became a helpless child
Hungry, thirsty, cold,
In need of our human love.
Oh the overwhelming mystery,
You, Lord, came searching for me!
You who kindled myriads of stars,

And call them all by name,
Open our eyes that we may see!
For until you make our heart of hearts your home,
We shall be for ever lost and alone
You who shepherd us to the almighty Father Maranatha
Come Lord Jesus.

Alleluia - Why Are We Here?

Our purpose is to praise!
No matter how dark the days.
Like a lark in shadow flies
To catch the new sun rise
Upon its outstretched wing
Rises up only to sing and to amaze.
For He, in darkness
Stretches out His wounded hands
To save us from our darkened minds
To give us His peace.

Aubade

As the high "chink chirrup"
Of bird song
Spins silver in the darkness
So light is heard before
It blesses the eyes
With longed for sight.
Pouring like wine and oil from a golden spoon
To feed us in the night.
So the word
Was prophesied
To lonely exiles
Until the star was kindled
When light itself in infancy
And might
Cried
For the joy he found in us!

Before Sunrise

In the hush before the dawn
when the sun crouches
below the horizon
like a lion
ready to spring –
I lie listening
to a little bird
talking to itself,
alone in the misty tree.
The sky grows pale
as the stars fly away
And the grass is wet through
as if it had cried all night long.

Black Swans Asleep, Noon

It is noon in sunny Spring
and full of singing birds,
While on the lawn
two black swans are sleeping,
dark and sooty as mid-winter night
in their soft ebony feathers.
Two dark silences
curved side by side
in secret parentheses.
But if they should sing!
They would put
all other songs to flight.

Carol

The young king comes
Before the spring comes.
Across the deserts of time
In the darkest night.
Riding on a donkey
Beneath the heart of May
While angels spread
Their silken wings
Before His hidden feet.
God's living love-token
To heal and to be broken
Comes to be born in Bethlehem.
To make himself a home in every heart.

Cathedral Mass

The slanting lance of sunlight
pierces the blue stained glass
and splashes in split prismatic light,
bleaching the candle flame white.
Then the bread is raised,
the new-born Son is praised
and, in the gilded cup (is lifted up)
He dies, shedding love's blood
in unending Sacrifice.

Christmas Journey

Driving down south
The eve of the birth of the lamb,
Comfortably we come
Motoring in the moth-like dusk we glide
Warmly wrapped in webs of music
Spun between the dazzling moving lights
Where others ride
We come to the "cold as charity" City of Lights – and lost children.
I fix my eyes on the one speechless star
Pinned like a talisman alone
on the dark soft breast of the weeping night.

Country Churchyard In Spring

Wood smoke hangs like incense
Over the still stones
Flowers from family and friends
Make each remembered grave an Easter.
Where they thirst and fade
The tall yew trees
Where the years forget.
Velvet lichens hide old names
While king cups blaze brighter
Than Pentecost flames
It's all a sunny wonder.
High in the naked trees
The mating birds
Sing their glittering challenges
Under a sky
Blue as forget-me-nots.

Cut And Thrust

Marriage is impossible.
I cut at you with the flint
of my disillusion,
trying to carve you
into my "ideal".
But you don't cry
or bleed
or even shout.
Are you then
as hard as me?

Dark Summer Day

At long last the rain-washed
bluebell sky glitters with the sun.
Little clouds sail high
in wisps of white wool
pulled from wet fleece.
Restlessly the wind tugs at the trees,
And already a few frail leaves fall.
The air is autumnal,
heady and cool –
Yet just to live in such light
is great pleasure
after such loud storms.
Gladly little birds call
"Come out to play, it is almost warm!"
The seasons are in a great race,
so try to treat each day as a treasure,
Golden, or silvered with grief.
Patiently.
That is the way
to Grace.

Dream Picture

Up and down the yellow sand
runs a small boy, spade in hand,
Waving his arms
at big white gulls
in brilliant sunshine,
Where ocean furls
its soapy, slippery sky-blue wave.
He's king of the castle
(and very brave).

His hair is just
the colour of sand,
He's sleeping with a seashell in his hand.
The ocean rocks him
strong and deep,

O sailor mine,
so fast asleep.

Epiphany
(Written on the day of my father's death)

O it is a long, long journey
To find the new young king.
No matter how brightly the stars shine
Or how sweetly the angels sing!
The desert crazes us with thirst
And the mountain path is steep.
Yet God – yes God Almighty
Loved us – at first,
And there he is asleep.

We've travelled far
And the gifts we brought
To give the king are lost!
We've tried so hard
What we had we shared
To keep hope alive at any cost
It seems to me
That the mystery of love is so very deep to see!

God, yes God Almighty loves us!
Just loves us!
And here he is
Asleep.

Evensong

When silence and the evening altar
spreads gold upon the grass
The winged breezes
Lift the air before us as we pass.
When birds flock homewards
o'er fields dappled with the dew
Our worried hearts flock home
towards love's candle shrine and you.
Where tired hearts reach out
towards love's meaning in the mind
Of God, beneath the veil of bread
The home of human kind.
Where crumbs of comfort
heaped upon our thankful hands are lifted
We feast on love alone,
O how greatly we are gifted.

Finches

I went into the aviary
where tiny yellow finches
fluttered and flickered
like flames
from branch to branch
under the transparent roof.
These birds were shards of sunlight
and at nightfall
These atomies
surely return
into the yellow sun
to keep it warm.

Good News

There is a way out of chaos
Even the chaos we make for ourselves,
When in our bitterness
And selfish pride we pull our house down about our ears.
Jesus is the answer to chaos
We cannot dig our way out of the rubble our tyrannies make,
He comes.
We only have to be still and humbly ask.
He comes – the workman.
Digging us out of our perilous self-induced disasters.
He is there before me entering into my death
Taking the weight of my hate
On his heart
And feeding me with his body
His blood
And his breath.

Harvest

Mary holds her dead son
spread out overflowing
As a sheaf of grain in her arms.
His blood is splattered and scattered
Like poppies in the corn.
Precious remedy for all our pain.
"Here come and eat" she calls
"He is dead, dying for you all
To become your bread
Hear my crying.

Here is your ransom
From death everlasting!
You are born in his blood
You are all my children now.
For him, he gave me
Dear John to be my own son
But I call to you all
This mystery of love cannot be confined.
In this pain he burned to refine you.
Here he displayed forgiven
Given for you who betrayed him
He is the way to heaven
Allelujah!"

Hesketh Park Lake

The summer trees in rich tresses
hang around the pool;
Or as fine lace shawls of green,
red and pale yellow -
Where the delicate willows fall,
dabbling their long fingers
as the breeze blows cool.

High piles of pointillist leaves
are strung as if on fine wires,
Hush, Seurat, Seurat
that stretch out to catch
their chameleon reflections;
One moment brown, then green,
then yellow
as the autumn sheaves.

The silky water glitters,
stroking the smooth pebbles,
deep, deep down -
Where silvery fish slide silently
chasing their shadows in the sun.

The ducks are so comical!
Like tiny, painted slow rowboats,
their little hidden feet
paddling madly
as they draw long white triangle wakes -
Then bob their bright beaks down
But do not drown.

High Rise

The jungle is all around us
And isolation another hope
Terrifying mountains of loneliness
Those high rise flats
Crushing whole families under ice
Glaciers of "this is ours"
Fear bars all the doors
Broken bottles thrust into unguarded faces
Fingers twist into fists
Love goes sour in the heat of greed poisoning need
You have to be tough
To scale these heights
A fearless mountaineer
To brave and bear
This close-packed anonymous loneliness.

Lines

You walk out of the door
silent, drowned in my words,
Walk out to work, snail-like
carrying the house
and me inside.
Then you come back to me
across the desert of the day.
O then let me be
quiet and still as water,
wordless and clear,
No longer contradicting
your heartbeat
with my bitterness.

Magpie

Flung like a dark gage
at the window, challenging.
Black and white
fashionable glove –
Flapping,
Chattering,
Oh SO clever,
"Pica, pica!"
Oh so smart!
You can be taught to speak,
But we –
Great lolloping, earth-bound
human beings
Cannot fly –
And often,
Cannot even be "human".

Mea Culpa

The bars of their prisons
Are in my mind,
The Molotov cocktail is under my tongue,
The sjambok lash is in my hand
And all the Intifada stones.
Who can break down the prison walls?
Who can take the fire from my mouth?
Who can take the lash from my fist?
And the stones?
Only the child can break the bars,
Only God's flame can burn out my rage,
Only He who was flogged for me – can take the lash away.
He gives us his heart for our stones.

Mid-wife

Learning to listen
may come too late.
Frustrated feelings
can boil into hate.
If you answer my questions
and question my answers
too soon
My inner being will be distorted,
cruelly aborted,
never to be known.

Memento Mori

The sun is a fine honey light
Hanging in the turning trees.
Brightly each leaf glows
Red as blood
Flowing down the breeze
Like tears wrung from lonely years.
Every distinct and separate grief
That time can never ease
Each leaf brims out
With a summer so fire
The sun itself is enchanted.
Late autumn is a haunted time

Stretched out upon the branches
God's only son – the vine itself.
Thirsting on His tree
Which flows for you and me.
For He is victorious
In our fight.

Morning Call

I am plunged before I wake
Into a cold shower of sound.
All the birds of Oxfordshire
In full song.
Cascades of glittering music
Into this moth-grey, lamp lit morning
While on the wall above my head
The fingers of passing cars
Write silently "move on".

November Circle

(Frank's favourite, written in the "Lyrical Landslide")

Now is the time of the golden fleece
when rubies litter the lawn,
When shallow puddles sheath with ice
and berries burden the thorn.

When smooth green fields are seas of mist
and trees are skeletons dancing,
Time of the dead when winter dread
is cheered with the spring's advancing.

November Evening

The sky above the roofs
so blue, so calm,
The first faint blush
of evening –
Pale hearts ease colour,
deepening into violet
for remembrance,
With just one perfect star
pulsating bright,
Waiting for the moon
that borrows the sun's light
to burn and bend
its fickle bow.

November Rainbow

There are arabesques of silver seagulls
bright against the dark back-drop
of a November squall.
The heavy clouds lumber along
like proud dowagers
that tear their petticoats
on the spiky trees
and show off their snowy lace.
Then a blue silk scarf is thrown
as the yellow sun brazenly pushes
the dark drapery aside
to mate with its silver reflection
in the rain,
making a rainbow.

O May Marie

(May 1990...inspired by events in Lourdes at this time)

O May Marie with blossom-bowed trees
Warm as an embrace
And full of graceful flowers,
What wonders were at work in you
In this mild month so long ago?
This wild world's maker
Came to regain our peace
To be slain by us, no less!
And arose victorious.

Out of The Depths

Stand by my side
Then the darkness is divided.
Curtains open wide
When I know that we two
Have decided
To wait upon the Lord
Who was so cruelly crucified.
Our fears tell us lies
Our pains perplex us.
Like a swarm of bees
Our sins sting and vex us.
The devil is jealous
Of our trust in the cross of Jesus.
For he knows that no matter
How much he tries to ensnare us
Christ Jesus will free us
Maranatha.
Christ calls us to enter his broken heart
Come to him
Receive God's reprieve.
His love alone cancels out our sinful pride.
Stand on the word.
Come follow Jesus Christ
For he is victorious.
Loving, living in us!
God's kingdom will come!
We have been given a great new start.
Maranatha.

Owl

From a cage the long-eared owl
watches me as I move around him.
Unblinkingly he stares
with his huge eyes fixed on me,
cold as cryptic gun-sights.
He is hunting me!
I try to laugh at him
but I am unnerved.
How dare he stare me out?
But I run, like a rabbit –
away –
Wondering if his head
came off!

Presentation

Oh Jesus, my love
God's only Turtle Dove,
Named in the womb by an angel
Carried by Mary into the temple
And presented to God never to be reclaimed.
Now He is named
Not to be bought back
By the blood of sparrows
Oh man of sorrow.
So soon you begin your task
Yet we have the temerity to ask
Why does He let us suffer?
When you, holy one
Continually offer your love
And never swerve once given
Until we reach heaven.

Reflections - The Necessary Ingredient

I stand stirring my husband's cup
And stare through the dark bleak window
Into the drizzle dazzle of the winter evening.
And see me
Bitter and empty – staring back.

I stare at the closely stacked
Lighted mysteries.
Along the long lines
Of darkening suburban streets,
Wondering what stories of love or hate
Wait behind the glowing blinds
Of these hard backed houses.

To there, another wife or mother
Wondering if she can add
The necessary sweetness
Of adventure and romance
To her hero's tea?

Silently I stir
Trying not to see
The tense tired eyes
That glance warily at me.

Sweetness is so easy
To add to tea.
But it is hard
To be warm and simply waiting
Wordlessly.

Sea Changes

At night the shingle rattles
under the sea-shore window
like coins in my begging bowl,
While under the hissing
white tongues of the waves
The sea's throat
is smooth and seductive as silk.

In the dawn I go down to the beach
looking for fossils of driftwood
for my dead fire,
And dare to write our names
again and again together
with my frozen fingers.

Then I look across the sand far, far out.
Where is the sea?
Have you taken that away with you too?
No, there it glitters like a broken window-pane,
tearing me again and again,
Leaving me with only
your name in the dull gold at my feet.

Sky Picture

In the late afternoon
the white fleecy clouds
blush like rose petals,
Roses and gold – afloat
on a calm blue lake.
And where the clouds
retain their virgin snows,
They change into
mountains of ice
In faery lands
of long ago.

Short Leave (Country Matters)

Please walk with me at dawn
across the tangled meadow
where bright butterflies shimmered dance.
Sit with me at noon on the gate
in the May tree's shadow,
watching waves through the wheat fields advance.
Follow me at night through the wood,
I know a place that is good
with wild berries for our food,
where our white steeds can prance.

Stretch out at my side in starry eventide
where the grass smells like mead,
And say to me, even if it is a lie,
that it is me, only me, you need!
(Stay with me, don't go back,
Dear Soldier Jack, don't go back
to the war, far in France).

Then he fell asleep a little while in my arms
as I held him safe from all harms.
When he screamed with awful terror in a dream
he looked at me with eyes of flame
but he did not know my name,
And he shook with dreadful sobbing
For dead comrades he had loved.

Then he fell asleep again,
I just held him, child and man.
And I wish now
he had always slept like that
and I had never moved.

St Martin's Summer

Is there enough gold on the trees
to buy back the days,
the days of summer?
See where the autumn shimmer
shifts and shivers in the breeze –
What bright wonder
above and under us
rustles, whispering
"Plunder us – take your fill
of all the colours you can name
Until your inward eye
is sated with light's mystery,
Then in the cold coming winter days
our flame will kindle your heart
and keep you warm".

The Colour of Prayer

Tell me, what is the colour of prayer?
Is it gold or blue as summer air,
Or black as sorrow
or silver as tears
That fade with the morrow
as the new dawn appears?

Is it red as the blood that ransomed us all,
Or brown as the bricks in the churchyard wall,
Is it yellow as jealous gold for which Judas betrayed,
Or purple as the robe that the Master arrayed?

Oh, wind me a rainbow
that blesses the land!
The colour of prayer?
The Lord understands.

The Coming

Translucent roses of purest white
Tremble in the December mist.
Memories and promises closely enfolded
Doubly precious they cling to the light.
Snowy light resembling their angel beauty
Look – look again.
Prophesying love's pain – the thorns also are there,
Love comes to share
And the thorns are the chosen crown of Christ.

The First Frost

I have lost a precious joy –
Bird song at eve and dawning,
first gold of every morning
that taught my heart to pray.
Not all my tears
though many the years
will buy them back –
And though I lie stretched taut
as fiddle strings
my sense no longer sings,
my cup is dry –
My thirst is like a pain:
Must I have ears in vain?
No. I must sing on and on
and like the swan
singing – die.

The Friendly Goose

I visited a bird sanctuary one day
in early spring –
And all around me
I heard the singing birds.
Then a comical long-necked
web-footed goose
called insistently to me,
(but not in English
so I did not understand a word).
It padded after me
protectively,

My chaperone.
Introducing me to all the ducks
and making me feel
quite at home.

The Lord Is My Shepherd, I Lack Nothing

In meadows of green He lets me lie,
to the waters of repose. He leads me,
there He revives my soul.
He guides me by paths of virtue
for the sake of His name.
Though I pass through a gloomy valley
I fear no harm;
Beside me your rod and staff
are there to hearten me.
You prepare a table before me
under the eyes of my enemies;
You anoint my head with oil,
my cup brims over.
Ah, how goodness and kindness pursue me
every day of my life;
My home, the house of the Lord,
as long as I live.

They Come Home

They come home.
When I kneel all alone
in a silent church.
I see them fill up empty pews.
From Flanders, from Falklands
in drab uniforms,
they are here, loving,
willing us safe from
all harm
in a freedom we dare
To abuse.

Victory

Worship the Lord in fear and trembling,
Serve the Lord without dissembling,
Praise the Lord with loving, grateful hearts.
Seek His word above all others,
Through Grace he makes us his brothers
called in love.
His Holy Kingdom starts - where?
Right here in me,
Christ has set me free
laying majesty aside
adorning us! The Church His bride
"Heaven above cannot contain me,
Give me your heart I will sustain thee
though all the ages I have called your name.
There was one way for me to save you
Upon the cross, see, I forgave you.
Forgive each other - truly from your heart.
Let my Holy Kingdom start - where?
Right here, in you!
Prove my promise to be true
For I alone can give you liberty,
Love me and life will never be the same."

Willow

The willow is a waterfall of light,
that pours in glittering, pensive waves
over the silken, rain-wet grass.
Where white daisies shine like the stars
until the silver evening star appears,
When they close up their yellow eyes.

York Minster

The heavy door thuds behind me
leaving me, suddenly, blind and deaf.
I feel the stone forest
arching above
up, up into the heady secret gloom.
Stately stone trees arise
as I let the very colour of silence
fall, soft as breathing, into me.
Soon I can see the light!
Rainbowing from lancet windows
it comes, singing into the stone
before the choirs sing.
Visitors, whispering like leaves
are hushed in this autumn fall of gold
around the stone-shrouded dead;
When a trapped sparrow
pitifully sings
"Remember the living,
give us bread".

Autumnal

My tree is dressed in light today,
it stretches its glowing arms
out to me as if it knew me.
The tree shimmers,
light kindles the gaunt, black branches
where only a few leaves remain –
But each one of them shines –
As if lamp-lit from within.
Suddenly I am a child again
standing here
rooted in wonderment
which is where I begin.

("In my end is my beginning" – motto of Mary, Queen of Scots).

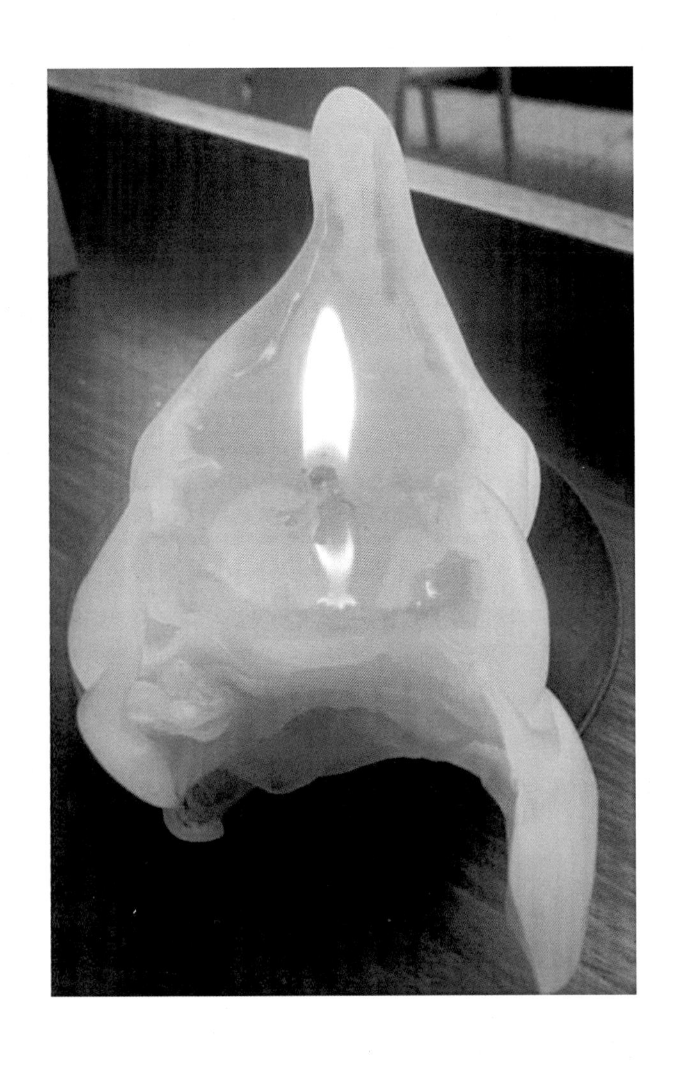

Index Of First Lines